1 A bad dream

Somewhere a telephone was ringing. Howard could hear it in his dream, but it didn't wake him up. It was dark in his dream, dark and terrible.

He was running, but it was like running through deep water. There were trees all around him, trees which tried to stop him. They reached out with their branches. And it was behind him. It was coming nearer. He wanted to shout for help. He was opening his mouth wide. But there was no sound. He could hear the noise it was making behind him – the heavy feet, the heavy breathing.

He was terrified. He looked behind . . . He could see it! He could see the burning eyes, the yellow teeth. Oh, no! It was coming nearer. A few more steps and then . . .

The telephone was still ringing. 'Don't answer it,' Howard shouted.

Suddenly he was awake. His body was hot and wet. The bedclothes were nearly off the bed. He was awake and safe. It was only a dream! He tried to pull the bedclothes back onto the bed. But something was wrong. His arm felt strange. He lifted his head, and looked. Beside his bed, there was a metal pole.

1

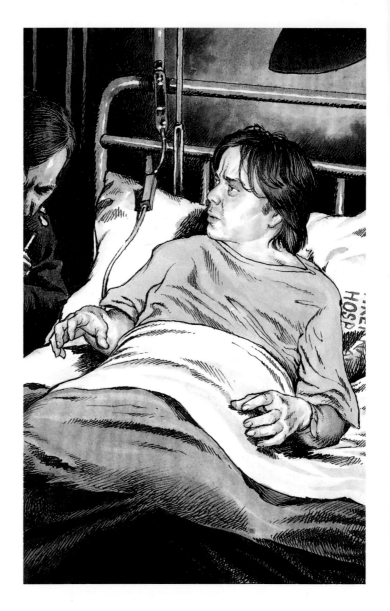

There was a tube coming from it. His arm was tied to it. He let his head fall back on the bed. Then he knew what it was. He was in hospital. But why?

He was probably a patient. He was ill, or hurt. Maybe he had been in an accident. He tried to think, but he couldn't remember. This happened sometimes after accidents, people said. You forgot what had happened just before, but . . . Howard felt cold around his heart.

He couldn't remember anything . . . not the accident (but was it an accident?), not the hospital, not his home, or family (did he have a family?). He couldn't even remember his name.

Who was he? He didn't know.

He lifted his head again and looked to the right. He was in a hospital ward, a long room full of beds and other patients, men who were sleeping or reading. At one end he could see a nurse. She was speaking into a telephone. Was that the telephone he had heard?

He looked to the left and he became still with fear. A man was sitting on a chair just by his bed. There was something in his hand, a magazine or a book. His head had fallen forward and he was asleep. Who was he? What was he doing here, beside Howard's bed? Was he a guard? The man seemed to feel Howard's eyes on him, because he lifted his head, stood up and looked down at Howard.

'So you're awake, Mr Blake,' he said, and his voice was ugly. 'Have you had a good sleep? How's your head?

Is it still hurting?'

'Who are you?' said Howard. His voice was very quiet. 'What am I doing here?'

'You've had a little accident,' the man said. 'There's someone here who wants to speak to you.'

Howard closed his eyes. Yes, his head did hurt, but it hurt inside more than outside. Why couldn't he remember? What was happening? He didn't understand.

When he opened his eyes, two people were standing by his bed, his guard and another, older person. It was a woman with brown hair and cold grey eyes, wearing a dark blue suit. They were both looking serious, almost angry. But why were they angry? Were they angry with him? They closed the curtains around his bed and came inside.

'The Inspector wants to speak to you, Mr Blake,' said the guard.

The Inspector? Then these two were police officers. Had he been in a road accident? No, Howard knew this wasn't right. Police inspectors didn't worry about road accidents. They were too important. Then it was a crime! Perhaps . . . perhaps he had been attacked by a thief!

'Now, Mr Blake,' the Inspector began. Her voice was pleasant but it sounded cold.

'Why do you call me "Blake"?' said Howard. He had suddenly felt this was wrong. 'My name isn't Blake. It's . . . it's . . .'

'Come on, Mr Blake,' the Inspector said angrily, 'we know all about you. Why don't you just answer our questions? You'll have to, in the end.'

Howard was feeling more and more worried. He wanted to answer their questions, but he could remember nothing.

'What do you want to know?' he said weakly.

'What time did you arrive at the house in Primrose Avenue?' the Inspector said. Her voice was now hard and quick. 'How did you climb to the window? What weapon did you use to hit the old lady? What were you going to do with the green dragon?'

'Stop! Stop!' cried Howard. He felt sick. He couldn't breathe. He could only hear those last words, 'the green dragon', 'the green dragon'.

Howard groaned. The green dragon! Those eyes . . . those burning red eyes! And then he remembered more. Red eyes, red blood. A pool of blood on a Chinese rug . . . But he was the one who was hurt. He was the one who had been attacked, violently.

The detectives – of course, they were detectives – began to ask their questions again. They were hard questions. They were impossible to answer.

'I can't . . . I can't . . .' said Howard. 'It's no use. I can't remember.' He felt like a little boy. He wanted to cry.

'You climbed into the old lady's house in the dark. She heard you and went to look. You hit her when she got to the stairs,' the guard said.

And then the nurse was standing beside them. 'That's enough,' she said angrily. 'He's too ill to answer any more questions. You'll have to leave.'

She did something to Howard's arm. He felt himself sinking into sleep. The green dragon, the telephone, the pool of blood, the old lady . . . What had happened? He didn't know. But he was certain about one thing.

'My name's not Blake,' he said, loudly and clearly. Then he slept.

---

2 Escape!

Howard was still afraid when he woke up. It was night and the long ward was silent. Yes, he was still afraid, but he was stronger, much stronger. Something was going round and round in his head. It was something the detective had said, just before the nurse came.

He looked around the room. Everyone was sleeping. He could see the moonlight on their beds. Moonlight! That was it! The guard had said 'in the dark'. But he was wrong. It wasn't dark. It was moonlight, bright moonlight.

Howard sat up in his bed. He suddenly felt excited. Was he remembering at last? But his thoughts were gone before he could catch them. He wanted to shout with anger, but he had seen something. His arm was free. The pole and tube had gone and the curtains were open. Then he noticed something else. The guard was not there!

Howard tried to control his thoughts. What did he know so far? An old lady had been killed, an old lady who lived in Primrose Avenue. And the police thought *he* had killed her. That name, Primrose Avenue, he'd heard it before. Was the answer there? Could he find the address if he was free?

Free! He had to get free. He had to escape from the hospital. He had to discover what had really happened, because he was certain he had not killed anyone. He hadn't . . . he hadn't done that terrible thing. Then he lay back on the bed. He was feeling weak. How could he escape? They had taken away all his clothes.

Suddenly Howard heard voices outside the ward. He shut his eyes quickly, and lay very still. He could hear the voices of his guard and the nurses. The big doors opened and they came in quickly. They were pushing a stretcher. A man was lying on it. He was groaning.

'It was just outside the hospital,' the nurse was saying. 'He walked in front of a bus.'

They put the new patient on the bed next to Howard's. Doctors and nurses were all around him. Then one of the doctors said, 'We'll have to operate,' and the man was taken away again on his stretcher.

'I'll go and phone his wife,' said the guard, and left the ward. Then it was quiet again.

Howard didn't move for a very long time. Then slowly he opened his eyes. The ward was quiet. The other patients were sleeping again. He lifted his head and looked at the next bed. The man's clothes were still on the chair by his bed. They had forgotten to take them away. He wanted to laugh!

Howard got out of bed and stood up carefully. For a moment he thought he was going to fall. He shook his head. Then he felt all right. He smiled to himself. He felt strong. He could do it. Now he knew he could do it. He could escape!

He dressed in the bathroom. The man's clothes were a little too small but he could get them on. He looked at himself in the mirror. Now for the difficult part . . .

3 Inside the old house

But he was lucky. He saw nobody, and nobody saw him. He walked quickly out of the ward and out of the hospital. Outside, he saw that one of the nurses had left her bicycle against the wall. Howard stared at it. He had a strange feeling that he had done all this before. Somehow, a bicycle was important. But why? He couldn't remember. But he knew he could ride a bicycle. He shook himself, got on the bicycle and rode away quickly.

Somehow he knew the way. It was like having a map

in his head. There was Primrose Avenue, and there, yes, there was the big old house. It was hidden behind trees.

Howard started to walk up the drive. It was like the dream. He knew the way exactly. He was certain the answers were here, the answers to all of his questions.

Suddenly, he jumped into the shadow of the trees and stood very still under the branches. He could hear voices. He looked out slowly and saw a van, a white van. It was parked outside the house. Two people were standing by it. They were talking. They were wearing dark uniforms. Then he saw who they were. The police! Of course! A woman had been murdered in this house, and the police were guarding it. He had to be more careful. He had to go round to the back of the house. Nobody would be able to see him there. He crept through the trees silently. He stayed in the shadows.

Again, he knew the way. Here was the back of the house and here was the drainpipe beside the balcony. He climbed up easily and opened the window. Somehow he knew it wasn't locked. He climbed in and stood in the dark. He was breathing deeply, but he wasn't afraid. The house felt warm and friendly. He felt his way across the upstairs hall with his hands. Then he started down the stairs, step by step, slowly and carefully. Suddenly he felt afraid . . . very afraid. But why?

The house didn't feel friendly any more. Something was waiting for him downstairs, something evil and cruel and . . .

Howard cried out. He was terrified. Someone was lying on the floor below! He could see a white shape, with the arms out at the sides.

Then the moon appeared from behind a cloud and shone through the window. Howard's legs felt weak. The body he had seen on the floor had seemed real. Was he remembering something or was he just dreaming it?

He could see clearly now. It wasn't a body on the rug below. It was only some white marks. The police had made white marks on the floor. They had wanted to show the place . . . the place where the body had been. There was nothing to be afraid of, but had he remembered something else? He looked again, nearer and nearer. Then he turned away. He was feeling sick. Beside the shape of the head, the rug was dark, dark with blood.

Howard almost fell down the last steps. He ran across the hall. He crashed into tables, chairs and a large, heavy wooden box. The moonlight shone on its top. It was covered with Chinese dragons. He turned away. He couldn't breathe. He had to get outside. He had to get into the cold night air.

Suddenly he stopped. Voices! He heard the sound of a key in the lock. He looked around wildly. He had to hide, but where, where? The Chinese box . . . ? No, not there, not with those dragons! But he had to. There was nowhere else. He climbed in.

12

The voices came nearer and stopped just by the box. It was the two police officers Howard had seen outside. In the box he tried to breathe quietly. The voices were clear.

'I want you to have a look around,' one was saying. 'You haven't been here before, have you?'

'What happened exactly?' the other said. 'The old lady was murdered and . . .'

Howard thought about the police officer. Was he pointing to the shape at the bottom of the stairs, pointing to the dry blood?

But now he was speaking again, 'We've got the man that did it. You know that, don't you? He wanted to steal that dragon. We think the old lady heard something. Maybe she was watching television. She came to the bottom of the stairs. He was coming down silently and when he saw her . . . crash! He hit her. We don't know what he hit her with. He just hit wildly in the dark and ran back upstairs, and got out through the window. But this time he made a mistake. He slipped and fell.'

In the box Howard was listening very carefully to every word. Was he hearing the true story now? He thought carefully. Why couldn't he remember? '. . . in the dark', the police officer had said. No, that was wrong. It wasn't dark. But how did he know this? Why was it important?

'The cleaner found him the next morning. He was unconscious under the balcony. He was sleeping like a

14

baby, but he'd hurt his head. The dragon was on the ground beside him.'

Their voices were getting weaker. They were going away. Howard waited . . . fifteen minutes, twenty minutes. Then he opened the top of the box a little. Everything was still outside, still and dark. The moon was hidden again. He climbed out. He tried to be very quiet.

The room was very dark, and he couldn't see anything. He held his hands in front of him and moved one foot slowly, then the other. If he could switch on the light, just for a minute, he would be able to see the shape of the room . . . and the doors. His hands touched something hard. The wall! Good. If he followed the wall, he would find the door. Yes, here it was and here was the handle.

Howard suddenly felt light and happy. In a second he was going to be in the fresh air. And he was going to be free from the heavy walls of this house. They seemed like a prison to him now. He had to go to the police. He had to tell them they were wrong, terribly wrong about him.

He opened the door and stepped quickly through the doorway . . .

4 The green dragon

When Howard became conscious again, he was lying on a hard and dirty floor, and every bone in his body ached. He tried to move but the pain was too much. What had happened? This place was darker than upstairs. Upstairs? Then he remembered. He had opened a door and suddenly he was falling, crashing from step to step until he reached the bottom and . . . blackness.

'Just like the last time,' Howard thought. Then he sat up. The last time! Yes, now he remembered! He had been to this house before. He had seen the old lady. She was lying on the floor in a pool of blood but . . . did he kill her?

It had been about six o'clock when Freddy came. Howard was just finishing his tea. He groaned when he saw Freddy. Freddy was his brother-in-law and he had been married to Howard's sister, Helen, for nine years, but Howard didn't like him. He had never liked him.

He had always been suspicious of Freddy. He thought that Freddy wasn't really honest. He didn't know why he thought that, but he did. It was just something about Freddy. He didn't seem to have a job but he always had a big car and expensive clothes. Helen and the two children seemed to have everything they needed, but . . .

Howard got up when Freddy came into the room. Freddy was white and nervous. He went quickly to the window and looked out. Did he think someone else was coming?

'You've got to help me, Howard,' he said. 'I'm in trouble, bad trouble.'

Howard put down his teacup. 'What can I do?' he said carefully. You had to be careful with Freddy.

Freddy's hands were shaking when he lit his cigarette. 'I need money, a lot of money.' Howard started to speak but Freddy continued quickly. 'I know, I know. You haven't got any money. But you can help me.' He was looking at Howard nervously.

'How?' said Howard angrily. 'If this is one of your wild plans, the answer is "No". I'm not going to help you in any crime.'

'It's only a little thing,' Freddy said. He put out his cigarette. 'One phone call, that's all. There are some men . . .' He looked nervously out of the window again.

'What men?' said Howard. 'Criminals, you mean?'

'It's better if you don't know,' Freddy said quickly. 'They're not . . . gentlemen.' The word sounded strange, when Freddy said it. 'When they're angry, they're dangerous . . . very dangerous. They're going to . . .'

Suddenly Freddy covered his face with his hands. Howard saw that he was shaking and jumped to his feet. He put his hand on Freddy's arm. Maybe he didn't like Freddy but he was his brother-in-law.

17

18

Freddy looked up. He was terrified. 'You've got to save me, Howard,' he said. His voice was shaking. 'You're the only friend I've got. If they don't get their money soon, they'll . . . they'll kill me!' For a few minutes he could not continue. He was too frightened.

'If I'm killed, what will happen to Helen, and the children?' he whispered. He knew just how to hurt Howard. 'No husband, no father. Soon there'll be no house, no money. They'll be out on the street . . .' His voice was getting louder and louder.

'All right, all right,' said Howard. He was trying to stay calm. 'What do you want me to do?'

Freddy's plan was easy and it didn't seem dangerous for Howard. 'There's an old lady . . .' he began.

Her name was Miss Blake and she lived in a big old house on the north side of the town. The house was hidden behind tall trees. She had lived in the Far East for many years and when she came back, she was a rich woman. Her house was full of valuable things. Most of them were too heavy to move, but then there was the green dragon . . .

'Dragon?' Howard said. He laughed. 'What dragon?' It was made of green jade and gold, Freddy had told him, with red jewel eyes, and diamonds on its tail. It stood in a special place in her bedroom and it was lit by bright lights. He knew all about it, because he had been talking to her cleaner at the pub.

'It's worth thousands of pounds,' Freddy said. He was

excited now. He was enjoying this. 'Maybe hundreds of thousands. And it's light enough to carry, and small enough to hide!'

He wanted Howard to do one thing . . . just one thing. 'You phone the old lady,' Freddy explained. 'You tell her that a packet has arrived at your address, Primrose Road.'

'But this isn't Pr . . .' Howard began.

'I know, I know. You just say it's Primrose Road,' Freddy said quickly. 'Her address is Primrose Avenue – it's nearly the same, isn't it? You say your name is Blake, the same as hers. You say that the stamp on the packet says "Singapore" and inside it there is some special tea. You think there has been a mistake. You find her name in the phone book and decide the packet has come to the wrong address.'

He looked at Howard. 'Do you understand?' he asked.

'Yes, yes. Go on!' said Howard. He wanted to hear the end.

'Well, it's easy,' Freddy continued. 'You tell her you would like to bring the packet round to her house, but you can't walk, you're in a wheelchair. And you are just going away on three weeks' holiday. In fact, your daughter is coming soon to take you to the airport. Then you ask Miss Blake, would she like to wait three weeks or would she like to call round at your house immediately and get the packet herself?'

'But maybe she'll wait three weeks,' Howard said. He

didn't like the sound of Freddy's plan. But he was interested now.

'She won't,' said Freddy. 'She'll want her packet. She'll leave the house immediately because she'll want to catch you before you go. And I'll be outside her house. As soon as she leaves, I'll get into the house, I'll get the green dragon, and I'll get out. It'll be easy. It'll be like taking sweets from a baby.'

Howard felt unhappy. But what could he do?

'I'll bring the dragon back to you,' Freddy was saying now. 'You can hide it here.'

'Here?' Howard cried. He was frightened. 'Why here? What's wrong with your house?'

'The children,' Freddy said. He looked away from Howard's eyes. 'They may find it. Also, I want to hide it from those men. They won't look here.'

Freddy's plan worked perfectly. Howard was terrified when he heard the old lady's voice on the phone. He had hoped she would not answer. But she did. One hour later the green dragon was on his dining table. It was staring at him with those hot, red eyes. He hated it from the moment he saw it.

Howard had sat and studied the dragon for hours. He was drinking coffee, black coffee, and smoking cigarette after cigarette. At dinner time he couldn't eat. When he thought about food, he felt sick. Strange things were happening to his head. Once, with a shaking hand, he had touched the dragon again, but he pulled his hand

21

away quickly. It had seemed red-hot. 'I'm going crazy,' he thought. 'I will go crazy if I have to keep that thing much longer.' He lit another cigarette nervously.

Had someone seen Freddy, someone who knew him? Had those men – those dangerous criminals – been following Freddy? Had they seen him at Howard's house? The police had probably interviewed everybody who had worked for Miss Blake. Had the cleaner told them that she had talked to Freddy?

The questions went round and round in his head. 'I was stupid,' he told himself. 'Why didn't I throw Freddy and his crazy ideas out of the house?'

Suddenly he jumped to his feet. This had to stop. There was only one answer. He had to take the dragon back . . .

5 A body in the moonlight

Howard lay alone in the cellar below the house. He felt tired. But he felt better because he could remember the true story. It was like living through the story again, the fears, the terrible moments, like the moment when the police stopped him . . . 'Yes,' he thought, 'I remember . . .'

Very late that night he had taken the dragon back to Miss Blake's house. He had put it into his bicycle bag and had started to ride through the silent streets in the moonlight. Moonlight – that was unlucky. It had been dark earlier. Well, he couldn't do anything about that.

He had turned into Primrose Avenue . . . and there was a police car! The two officers in the car were immediately suspicious of this lonely cyclist in the early hours of the morning. They stopped him and asked what he was doing.

'I'm going to my mother's,' said Howard. He was shaking inside. 'They phoned me and said she was ill.'

The police officer wanted to help. 'Leave your bicycle,' she said. 'We'll drive you there.'

'No, no,' said Howard. He was feeling hot and uncomfortable. 'She's . . . my mother's house is just here, around the corner. But thank you. Thank you very much.'

He got on his bicycle and rode away. He heard the police car's engine. He didn't look back. The sound of the police car moved away. Howard breathed normally again.

A few minutes later he found Miss Blake's house. It looked strange and frightening in the moonlight. It seemed to be waiting for him. Was it a trap? For a moment Howard wanted to turn back but he told himself not to be silly. It was late. The old lady was asleep. He didn't need to be afraid.

Freddy had told him that he had dressed like a window cleaner and had climbed up his ladder to a balcony. The balcony led to the upstairs hall. He had planned to break a window but he found the window was open.

Now Howard saw the same window. He had no ladder but there was a drainpipe. He could climb it. Soon he was inside, and he was standing at the top of the stairs in the moonlight. He was looking down. He mustn't wake Miss Blake. He must leave the dragon somewhere. Perhaps on the table in the hall? He could see it below him. Then his heart froze in his body. There was someone lying at the bottom of the stairs! A body . . . a real body . . . and the moonlight was shining on the pool of blood.

And then he had run . . . back to the open window, to the drainpipe . . . The dragon was still in his hand! He started to throw it away with a wild cry. He slipped. The air was rushing past. The dragon was falling with him. Its eyes were staring, its mouth was open and its teeth were shining . . . Was it screaming, like him?

6 Guilty or not guilty?

'It wasn't a dream,' Howard told himself now, in the cellar. It really had happened. He had seen Miss Blake's body, but he hadn't killed her. She was already dead when he first saw her.

He thought about the dragon again. He could almost

see those red eyes shining in the dark. Then Howard went cold inside. There *were* eyes shining in the dark . . . here, in this cellar! They were watching him. Dragon's eyes? No, rats! He was terrified of rats. He felt around with his hands and found some pieces of wood. He threw them at the shining eyes, and shouted as loudly as he could.

Suddenly a voice came from above. 'Who's that? What's happening down there?'

It was a police officer. 'Help me,' Howard said weakly. 'Please help me.'

Later, the Inspector was sitting beside his bed. She looked serious, but happier. Howard was in hospital again, and he was clean and warm and comfortable. He was glad that it was all finished.

They knew who he really was – Howard Thomson. They weren't calling him 'Blake' any more. Howard told them everything. Well, nearly everything. He couldn't say anything about Freddy. He was thinking of his sister Helen and the children. He didn't want to hurt them.

'Yes, I stole the green dragon,' Howard told the Inspector. 'I tricked the old lady with my story about a packet of tea, and she left the house.'

'Oh, yes?' said the Inspector, and stared at him. 'We found a note. Miss Blake left it by the telephone. It said "Mr Blake, Primrose Road". Your story isn't quite true, is it? You tricked the old lady – yes. But she let you into the house that evening. She didn't leave the house. And when she tried to stop you from taking the dragon, you . . .'

'No, no! That's not true. It was afternoon, not evening.' Howard had to stay calm. He had to say he was the thief, not Freddy. He spoke slowly, carefully. 'She left the house in the middle of the afternoon. I went in and stole the dragon. That's what happened, Inspector. I didn't kill her. I couldn't kill anyone – she was already dead when I saw her for the first time.'

'Already dead?' the Inspector said quickly.

'Yes, I . . .' Howard saw that he had made a mistake. He had to explain. 'I went back that night,' he said.

'You went back?' The Inspector didn't believe him. 'Why did you do that?'

'I wanted to return the dragon, Inspector.' The words sounded weak and stupid. 'I was afraid of it, I don't know why, but it terrified me.'

'Oh, yes?' said the Inspector again, and looked hard at Howard with her cold, grey eyes.

She was silent for a long time. Howard tried to think of something. What could he say? He had to show the Inspector that he was not guilty of murder. But he could not find the right words.

'I suppose it's just possible,' the Inspector said. 'Perhaps the old lady went upstairs that evening and found the dragon was missing. Then perhaps she rushed to the telephone for help and fell down the stairs, and hit her head on the hall table at the bottom.'

'Yes, yes,' said Howard. 'That's it! She was killed by her fall. Don't you see, Inspector? I didn't kill her.'

The Inspector was still looking at him suspiciously. Howard thought hard. Somewhere there was an answer.

'But you were there,' the Inspector was saying. 'You say you went back to the house that evening. You were in the right place, at the right time, weren't you?'

Time!

Howard sat up and smiled. 'What time, Inspector?' he said. He was excited now. 'What time did Miss Blake die?'

'The doctor says it was about eight o'clock in the evening,' said the Inspector.

'When it was dark,' said Howard. 'When it was still dark. Before the moon had risen. But I was seen near her house in the moonlight – at two o'clock in the morning! If I was a murderer, I wouldn't go back there, would I, Inspector?'

'Who saw you?' said the Inspector, still suspicious. 'Friends of yours? I don't think I'm going to believe any friends of . . .'

'You'll believe these people, Inspector,' said Howard quickly. 'Two police officers in a police car saw me in Primrose Avenue. Right place, right time, Inspector!'

Howard felt pleased with himself. He lay back on the hospital bed and smiled. But the Inspector hadn't finished.

'I've got something here. I want you to see it,' she said. She opened a box beside her chair and lifted something out.

Howard's face went white. The Inspector was holding the green dragon in her hands.

'It doesn't look very important, does it?' she said.

The Inspector was right. Howard stared at the dragon. It didn't look important in the daylight. It looked cheap and ugly.

'It's not real, you know,' the Inspector was saying.

'What . . . what do you mean?' said Howard. He felt cold inside.

'The old lady sold the real one years ago. She wasn't as rich as people said. She needed the money. But the green dragon had some special magic for her, and she had this copy made.'

'You mean . . .'

'Yes. It's not jade and jewels. It's just plastic and bits of glass. You'd be able to sell it for £20, £25 if you were lucky.' She smiled. It was a very cold smile, Howard thought. 'It's not much money . . . not for five years in prison,' the Inspector added.

'Five years?' Howard said. His voice sounded weak and frightened. Five years in prison . . . and Freddy was going to be free!

'Well, four then,' said the Inspector. She smiled her terrible smile again, '. . . if you're lucky.'

Exercises to accompany this story are available on a photocopiable worksheet in the Storylines Teacher's Guide.

Oxford University Press,
Walton Street, Oxford OX2 6DP

Oxford   New York
Athens   Auckland   Bangkok   Bombay
Calcutta   Cape Town   Dar es Salaam   Delhi
Florence   Hong Kong   Istanbul   Karachi
Kuala Lumpur   Madras   Madrid   Melbourne
Mexico City   Nairobi   Paris   Singapore
Taipei   Tokyo   Toronto
and associated companies in
Berlin   Ibadan

OXFORD and OXFORD ENGLISH
are trade marks of Oxford University Press

ISBN 0 19 421947 X

© Oxford University Press 1996
First published 1996

This story was first published in the Streamline Graded Readers series.

Illustrated by Martin McKenna
Design and typesetting by Oxprint Design, Oxford
Series editors: Peter Viney and Bernard Hartley
Printed in Hong Kong